The Animal Within

Also by Rebecca Kavaler

The Further Adventures of Brunhild (1978)

Doubting Castle (1984)

Tigers in the Wood (1986)

A Little More Than Kin (2001)

The Animal Within

Poems By

Rebecca Kavaler

H \S

HAMILTON STONE EDITIONS

Acknowledgments

Some of these poems were first published elsewhere:

"O Pioneers" in *Fantasy & Science Fiction;* "Love at Fifty" in *Atlanta Review;* "That Summer" in *Hamilton Stone Review;* and "What My Mother Told Me" in *Prairie Schooner.*

Cover design: Claudia Carlson
Image: Pinar Yoldas

Library of Congress Cataloging-in-Publication Data

Kavaler, Rebecca.
The animal within : poems / by Rebecca Kavaler.
   p. cm.
ISBN-13: 978-0-9714873-8-3 (alk. paper)
I. Title.
PS3561.A8685A8 2008
811'.54–dc22

                       2007046914

To Edith, who was the prod
And Hal who played the god
Who made it so. And Sue, of course,
Who was so generous a resource
And to all those friends whose ears I bent
These poems are sent.

H \S

HAMILTON STONE EDITIONS
P.O. Box 43, Maplewood, New Jersey 07040

Contents

I

II

III

The Animal Within

I

Love at Fifty

Life gets tougher toward the poles.
Take the arctic:
Nothing there grows tall,
Reaches more than ankle-high.
Grasses lie low,
Even the trees crawl.
Craftiness is required
To keep alive.
The thaw
When it comes
Is brief,
Seeds must be ready,
No time for spring,
No slow gathering of intent,
No prefacing,
Summer roars in,
A torrent, a storm, a flash-flood
Of blossoming.
The ones that survive
Act as if it were
A once-in-a-lifetime
Event
As if there were
Never to be another.
Just so
We fell upon each other.

O Pioneers!

(Pioneer 10 spacecraft launched March 2, 1972, first destined
to leave solar system, carrying this identification plaque)

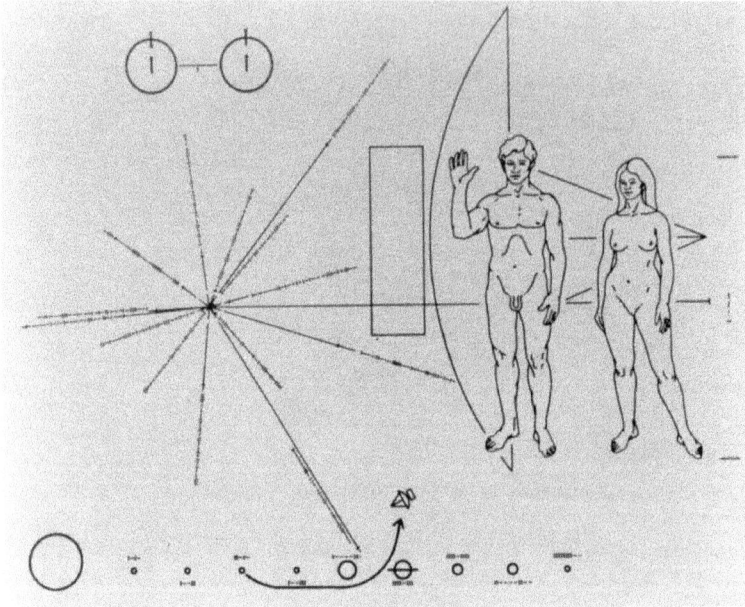

Does anyone still hang around the mailbox
Expecting a reply to that picture postcard
We mailed in seventy-two?
So airily, binarily we took a bow:
Hello, having wonderful time
Wish you were here. How
(And what) are you?

There we are, the two of us, standing
Side by side, our genitals exposed
To allay alarm.
Not to worry, we posture in our pride,

We come unarmed.
You have one hand raised in mock-Indian "How!"—
The salute white men have always given savages
When outnumbered. How friendly we look
Toward all aborigines, even toward each other
(We wanted to hold hands but were told
That would give the false impression we are one).
I, the smaller, with the suspicion of a cleft
Between the legs, am more retiring, my arms
Hang down relaxed, from which may be deduced
Your forelimb is not fixed permanently
In bent position (How!) but moves on hinges.
All in all, a portrait to evoke that wondrous cry:
O what a piece of work am I!

There was quite a fuss about the road-map, remember?
A slew of cassandras to wail
That a return address would call down
Fiery comets from the sky,
Unknown dangers on our head.
So we affixed our mark, Third-One-Out,
And showed the route: sharp turn to the left
Between that old gasbag Jupiter and
Saturn's dissolute rings and
On beyond the nudging of our sun,
The lion that rules us
(Beneficent despot but despot still,
Grown irksome as all despots grow in time),
Leaving behind the congestion of bright lights,
Trekking across immense prairies of stygian night
Toward a point midway between Taurus and Orion.
Surely a foolish path to choose—
Safe passage hardly to be found
Between the hunter and his prey.

So far not a word. Those attuned to wars
Turn elsewhere for their news.

What My Mother Told Me

Only money has enduring value, she said,
and removed her dentures.

I stare at the bed with its white chenille spread
at the effigy
the memento mori
my mother
resting in state on her catafalque.
She is already too thin to make a mound.

You are young, she accused me, you still believe
in the hegemony of the flesh
but I tell you the spirit is stronger
and the spirit is money,
waxing as the body wanes.

I never listen to my mother.
She calls them home truths
but I left home long ago.

Have you noticed, she rambled on,
how weightless money has become
since those early days of Yap stones,
of porcine jawbones?

It took no genius, I agree, to see the need
for something more portable.

Yes, she nodded, coins of shiny metal
engraved with the portrait of rulers,
something to bite down on.

She paused as if waiting for the antistrophe
or was it the rhetorical effect of pain?
Yes, I say, to assure her I am listening,
yes after so many years of no.

Nice jingle in the pocket, her thought
continued to pick its way
through the thicket of painkillers.
But cumbersome
in the carrying.

Paper is lighter, I agree,
though we have to take it on trust,
a hard reach for most of us.

And now, she capped me, we have
the pixelated ether
of the computer screen,
the animus, the breath of wind
that has been called our soul,
the spiritus sancti of our great amen.

I teeter in the doorway, half in half out
as I have always been in this house.
The first time I left I swore I would never come back.
When she leaves, she will be more steadfast.

Isn't it odd? she gummed, when money
grows at a compound rate, we call it profit
but when the flesh does the same
we use a nastier name.

I do not answer.
To what she has, the doctors say,
there is no answer.

When your father left me—she glared at me as if I were the cause—
I thought the world had ended. It had just begun.
Why is it that I could pass on to you intact
this accident of a face, length of bone, color of eye
but nothing of the life-wisdom I have acquired? That
would have served you better than your father's good teeth.

I thank my father for the teeth, clamp them shut.
It is not easy,

these constant flights, coast to coast, so close
on the heels of the sun that only two hours
will pass between departure and arrival.
From the moment I lift my baggage from the carousel
I feel the gravity of time standing still
much as I did as a young girl imprisoned here
on the top floor, a Rapunzel awaiting
rescue from a tower. I didn't have the hair
but I had the will.

What will become of you? was her dismissal,
you with your dead-end job and dead-end men.
(This old woman without her teeth still has a bite.)
I've given you good advice, not that you heed it.

You still have your looks but they will soon leave you.
Then you will see—her last words to me
as she turned off the light—
everything leaves you.
It's not that way with money:
it's you who do the leaving.

Executioner

Jackals feast on flesh
provided by other beasts.
We watch on TV.

He who throws the switch
believes that he serves mankind.
He loves his pet dog.

He's our holy fool,
so simple a heart. He kills
for us. It's his job.

Dysfunction

To everyone he meets he presents
a slice of himself–if not as introduction,
then as parting gift.

Easy enough to lop off what obtrudes:
no, not that, but lobe of ear,
tip of nose, fingers–five
from each hand–and don't forget
the toes: ten,

counting both feet.

Painful? Yes, I suppose.
But there is pleasure, however grim,
in beating them to the punch,
in making, as they say, a statement:
what a bloody mess they've made of things,

especially him.

In therapy–twice a week during lunch–
he blames his mother (that's me) whereas
his father, a serial killer as yet uncaught

gets off scot-free.

How Easy for the Child

How easy for the child to do those back-bends, how flexible his spine.

He draws with crayons his world, that terror incognito.

How easily he fills it with imaginary beasts. His stories move playfully as porpoises through the shoals of plot.

He grows taller, acquires a backbone that sees no point in bending. Travels to see the real world, but he's seen it all before, small on postcards, large on the screen. And what he learns, he already knows.

(Except love. Forget the movies, the books, the songs–particularly the songs, the hard rock, smooth ballads, nasal country. Nothing like this has happened before. He boasts of touching the stars.)

Then comes the day he can no longer touch even his toes.

Language

If not
for this pressing of air
through the chest,
this strumming of chords
in the throat,
this fricative of tongue
against teeth,

these gutterals
these nasals

to tear us apart,
to meld us with desire,
to send us out
as conquerors,
inventors
of wheels and wars,

where would we be?

If not
for this ability
to invest
brute sounds
with a thesaurus
of meanings,
to make
a dictionary
of hoots
and caws
roars
and hisses
clicks
and rumbles

what would we be?

Those other beasts
with saber teeth
armored plate
swaggering size
thought to
dominate

yet there they go,
losers in the race,
and it is left to us
to take their place

snarling
hissing
roaring

aping.

History Taking

All I want is those pills to take when I'm feeling low,
but how long have I had it, he first wants to know

It's hard to say. Since Christmas, I suppose,
but the truth is it comes and it goes.

Is it something, he presses, that afflicted my mother:
My father? *His* father? My sister or brother?

Is this a disease, I wonder, that he's trying to trace?
If so, he should include the whole human race.

Where does it hurt, he asks: here? here?
On a grade from one to ten, how severe?

I make the so-so gesture with a teetering hand, pain
not being something in which I have sought to attain

a perfect score. Describe it, he urges me then,
is it sharp, is it dull, intermittent, steady: When

is it strongest: in the morning or night?
Have I noticed if it affects my appetite?

It's dull in the mornings, I begin, hours can pass
when I don't feel a thing and I think at last

the worst is over, I can face what the future brings,
assured of being well again. But the evenings

ah! that's a different story. Not so good,
and when I happen to be in that neighborhood

and see him there
in the Blue Moon
closeted with her
in the same booth
we would lay claim to

it becomes sharp as that needle you just used to take my blood.

Iphigenia

Eyes soft as a doe's
Facing the hunter's taut bow
Uncomprehending.

She serves a purpose
Greater than herself—don't we
All? I kiss the knife.

They will sing of you
Through the ages, I tell her
And make the first cut.

I stand on the shore
Awash in blood, awaiting
A good wind for Troy.

Dateline Alamogordo, N.M.: July 16, 1945

I should have known
when you said my smile
was brighter than
                a thousand suns

I should have known
from the way you cast
your glance everywhere but
on my face that you were seeking
from day one a way to
                send me back.

But I am not the kind of
lover who goes in for
                one-night stands.

Urban Spring

Such valor in this
green
grass
cracking
the concrete
bearding
the sidewalks
trees
leafing
in trucks' exhaust
weeds
flourishing
in cellar doorways
below street level
under iron gratings
like the art
of children
in concentration camps.

Such brave contriving.

And these young girls
running
for the school bus
still taken by surprise
by the onset
of menses
(always a surprise
no matter how adept
mothers
at mothering,
issuing forewarnings
doomed
to be dismissed
as lies)
still uncomfortable
with the reality

of breasts
those foreign implants
on the flat plains
of their chests
whose bounce
must be constrained
by binding–
are they too
endowed
with that green

spirit of surviving?

That Summer

Sometimes language gets in the way
of what needs to be said.
Which accounts for these long silences.

I was sure of what I felt for you but
Putting it into words made it suspect.

That summer, lying in the grass, our bodies
spoke of openness and all asprawl
we listened to the sky.

Even that has lost some of its blueness
in translation.

II

Unlikely

as it once seemed that He would be so profligate as to play dice with the universe, no denying some game of chance was required . . .

As we know, nothing is worse than eternity for boredom.

So if not dice? Then settle for Sex: more than a card game to shuffle genes, rather a plot device to keep things moving beyond the banality of Eden

and while the world goes to hell, we two lie, legs entwined awaiting the knock, the cuckold's roar

the big bang.

To My Grandchild

I've brought you here all this way
to show you this landscape in which
timepieces melt and buildings peel,
to say this is where I was young,
I was young here.

The empty housing holds its breath, the streets
are traffic-lorn. We stand on once a hill,
short-memoried (only I still smell the pines),
cut off in its prime. Flat-topped now, graded
to an easy climb. I wonder if like an amputee
it sometimes feels the height no longer there as pain.

I trace for you the downward sweep
of old trolley lines buried in the tar pits
of ancient asphalt. You look around,
ready for some new adventure. Your hair,
from which childhood is not yet combed,
blinds like the sun's corona.

Here is where I spent my youth, I say. Spent.
A sour pucker in the mouth. I spit it out.
You squint into the light, incredulous at the view?
Then spin east north west south, taking it all in.
I take in you.

And then you run all the way down
without stopping
to the ice-cream truck
whooping it up like a cowboy
in from a long trail drive
shooting up the town.

Medusa

Throw a party, she'll be there,
dressed with thrift-shop elegance,
an eclectic style that suits her off-center beauty.
Her mouth, with its thin Irish smile,
is a bon mot in itself that other women
wish they had said as she plays the room
with the strobe light of her attention.
Snaky curls are all the fashion yet
there is something in her stare,
as well as in the way she wears her hair . . .

Her hands invigorate the lassitudinous air
as she tells her crowd of admirers
how depressed she is, how alone,
setting off a string of laughter
that pops like firecrackers
(none was ever so pretty
and none was ever so witty
in turning men to stone).
She cajoles, harangues,
entertains—my God, she entertains!—
with her despair.

Rooms of Childhood

The rooms of childhood are always small when revisited: low ceilings and flimsy floors and walls reeking of injustices never righted,

rooms still inhabited by tenants who failed to shrink in tandem with the walls, whose heads brush the roof beams when you open the door.

The brothers Grimm knew whereof they spoke when they filled their stories with giants, witches, children-eaters.

How we loved those fairy tales.

Fear of Flying

Those who are not afraid of planes
trust to metaphor, believing
they can fly in a direction contrary
to the sun's and return to find
the city has not crumbled
the children still waiting
at the airport.

No Great Loss

the concrete, the steel, the glass

that vulgar two-finger salute
saying fuck you to the sky
in the lingua franca of the New York cabbie

no great loss

(except for those smiling faces
plastered on fences, lamp posts,
endless walls, looking
so happy to be compacted
under twisted steel, dispersed
in concrete dust).

Yet when we see in background shots
in a film we are watching—say
a romantic comedy preserved on tape—
that double exclamation point—!!—in the skyline
we see why some thought them beautiful.
It is like looking at a photograph of ourselves
when we were young, feeling blessed
by the gods and deservedly.

Which If Not Victory Is Yet Revenge
—Paradise Lost

Ah, young Joseph, how high you hold your head.
Jewish-hard your eyes, Jewish-soft your mouth
And a high Jewishness of nose forbids all doubt
Of your noble state. No fancy coat. Instead
You wear handsomeness and youth with such an air
We know you are the father's darling, the only son
Of the only beloved. You are the dreamy one,
Teller of grandiloquent lies, self-anointed heir
To Pharaoh's kingdom. And because we are your kin,
Though lesser folk, we too must dream, interpret it
And bind you fast and place you in a pit.
Do not call us enemy. We are your friend.

The Wild Child

He thought, after so many years of hiding in the forest afraid of humans, to come into the open, naked as he was, and share this fervid buzzing in his head, the honey of his solitude.

He thought, after so many years, to brave the fierce conviviality of the two-legged creatures whom he resembled in form and must be his kin although they moved in herds and seemed to fear to be caught alone.

Hey there, he cried, here I am, let me hear the sounds you make with your tongue, touch that smooth hide, let me see how your body works unclothed. He entered their midst, arms outstretched—for weaponry, a smile.

But they looked at him and saw no one. However loudly he called out, he could not be heard. Like an image on film that had failed to acquire the timely fixative of their regard, he had disappeared, not to be retrieved.

Trees

> "Get That Oak an Accountant: Study Puts a Dollar Value on Work
> Done by City's Trees."
> *New York Times* headline, May 12, 2003

They've done a cost analysis on trees. Here are the figures on paper, charting the pollutants removed daily from the air: so many grams per tree of our lungs' exhaust, so many grams from the belching of our cars.

Then there's the oxygen they provide for us to breathe, so many grams per tree. Surely that's worth something. Not to mention the comfort factor of cooling the city in summer and muting gunfire in the streets.

I wonder if in coming up with that bottom line they factored in the fact that like the gods, trees were here before us.

And that they provide us with the wherewithal for crucifixions, that sine qua non of divinity.

Obits

That famous face (siren of the silver screen), a shock
to read that she is dead. I thought her dead long ago
and here I read of her cremation. *Esse est percipi?* If so,
I killed her first by starvation, the slow withdrawal of my
attention.

Death by newsprint is quicker, cleaner.

I never read the obits before John died, but I see now
this is where they hide the real news. She was ninety-two.
I skim her life, the marriages, the list of long-forgotten films.
Jump to the end. Who survived her? No one. Leaving no job here for a
therapist like mine to put a stop to grieving, to insist in her no-nonsense
voice enough's enough, time to mend.

Enough's enough. As if I'm pigging out on tears.

I tell her grief is all that's left of me. She pins on my lapel
a happy face, pats my behind. This is war, she chirps,
the photographs must go. I am not to see any film on which
he left his trace, not only those in silver frames but the loose ones
as well lost in the clutter of my drawer, smelling of my scent.
Office keys returned. Clothes to Good Will. Papers burned.
Books separated, his from mine, the ultimate divorce.
She swept through every room: Is this his? his? his?
What I would not give, she took by force and out it went.

John, John, I cried last night, and he appeared as when alive,
though marginally more dim—I had to fudge the face.
Eyes squeezed tight, I will the image to survive.
Good grief! he jokes with empty orphan annie eyes,
knowing grief is all that's left of him.

He swears to never leave me. I swear the same sweet lies.
He looks around this fumigated place. He is not blind.
He knows murder is what I have in mind.

Odd Couple

We are the odd couple to our friends, having stayed together
so many years, our infidelities, unremarkable at best,
now buried in a past that lends itself like all history
                    to be rewritten.

I am sure they look at you, see flab and paunch, thin straggle
of hair; look at me, see an equal devastation of the flesh.
How they must shudder at the thought of us naked in bed
                    mimicking our youngers.

They do not understand that awakening through the years
to the same unguarded face, totting up time in day-to-day
increments, we have grown old without noticing and see ourselves
not as we are but as we were: still young, still foolish, still doubting
                    this will last.

Proceedings of the Flat Earth Society

You think you've trapped the sun
on the horizon
red-eyed, engorged, impaled
only to watch

it slip away, hardly believing
the speed with which
it sinks below the tangent
of the earth,
slurped into the gullet
of the night.

Galileo, Copernicus, Christopher Columbus
were all wrong, you
are not so foolish
as to dismiss
the evidence of your eyes,
to insist it's you
who turn
and the world on which
you stand is round,

a theory so unsound
as to place us
on a wheel
requiring,
if we would keep
our ground,
the balance and the flippers
of a seal.

The Animal Within

Homage to Sir Thomas Browne

We, who supposedly contain all Africa and her prodigies,
are revealed for what we are only in the dying
when this flesh, once apostrophized as too too solid,
has proven renderable as any carcass and in the process
manufactured hollows where hillocks of cheeks once smiled,
then weeded out the overgrowth of hair to uncover
a tenderness-evoking curve of skull,
                a property we had thought
                only of the newly born.

The mirror reflects no longer a unique face but the template
of the race: uncles, aunts, cousins far removed, some ancestor
who left no trace in family history yet surfaces now like
a species long thought extinct hauled up from the ocean's depths
and when that dissolves what is left
                but the animal within
                which we made so much of.

Epitaph

Born unfinished, it took a year
before I walked,
two before I talked, six
before my brain-case closed,

in my teens before the x-rays
showed long bones
had hardened
to the breaking point and always

the landscape my eyes first opened upon
the most dear

the food first spooned into my mouth
the most savored

and when I died, the infant
in me was still
screaming.

III

Dreams

They say
> you never stop dreaming
> you just fail to recall.

For proof
> they track the shuttle of your eyes
> weaving phantasmagoria
> behind closed lids.

See, they say,
> the shape-shifting cast,
> the craziness of plot
> recorded in these needle-sharp spikes:

these here
> mark the car's downhill plunge
> (brakes have failed) and these the sly
> seduction on your parents' couch.

Here
> is your lost child crying in the fog
> whom just for a moment you forgot
> and here you are called before the class

where
> you recite some verse, naked in your pride,
> waiting for applause. Instead the teacher
> flays you with contempt, labels you fraud.

See, they say,
> there's a whole library here
> if you could but decipher the runic script
> or transverse this antique map

complete
       with serpents, turtles and furred men
       inhabiting a continent of fear
       bounded by oceans of rage.

But is a dream
       still a dream if there's nothing there
       when you awake, nothing to recount
       over morning coffee to your bored mate?

What profit
       has a dreamer if she gains the boon
       of unbroken sleep yet loses
       all her wild imaginings?

These days
       nothing remains of the nightwork
       of my mind—the panic, shame, lust—
       but what is imprinted on the tangled sheet.

I sleep like a log,
       is the boast of some who seek such oblivion.
       I am not one. I feel unleavened, made of
       heavier stuff than dreams are made on

He has the coffee poured. Sleep well? he asks.

Like a log, I say.

If Only

Timing is everything,
life being slapstick
a comedic turn, a farce
with doors opening
and shutting.

Take our first meeting,
both married
but not to each other.
If only.

Timing is everything:
Say we met sooner,
we could have married
each other, been divorced,
remarried by now
to someone new.

Instead there is still this yearning:
if only.

Coney Island. Winter

One lone man.
Joyless sands present
exclusive front
which only gulls frequent.

Beneath pier
water churns
toad-green in sleep
muttering
tooth-grinding
slime-deep

in dreams but out beyond
crabs and gulls
white as mad-dog saliva
waves reflect all light.

Behemoth twitches
wrinkling its skin.

Tide comes in.

Advances
like Jehovah's hosts,
meets the man
at water's edge.

He does not move his feet.

Black shoes
tight-laced, high-shined,
sink down.

Gustatory sucking
in wet sand.

Black hat, black coat
furled black umbrella—
pot-bellied
flat-footed
spindle-shanked
city dweller

small stockholder,
cantankerous investor,
backbone of the nation

a crank

who will not sign a proxy
in the present situation
but stands firm,
determined to oppose
by parliamentary motion

the Atlantic Ocean.

Dog in the Holocene

In the end it is the muteness that is unbearable.
Tail speaks, tongue licks, love pricks
But he must say it all by dancing on two legs.

Somewhere along that double-helixed strand
Is the hunter's imprint stiffening to perfect point,
A freeze-section of eloquence.

Otherwise it is mostly sleep
With rage like lust kept on the leash
And when sad do not eat.

My eye, swimming in its white, probes his,
Dark and moist with memory half-surfacing
But never seized:

Rotting furs blood grease
the homey stink of caves
MASTER

Now the smell of wax on highly polished floors.
Paws slip. He sprawls ludicrous in four directions.

He has no words to justify himself.

Creation Myth

Supposing now

God created the universe from notes scribbled in a chaotic frame of mind, the all but illegible hand of one who awakes suddenly from a deep sleep.

To better see, his first command: Let there be light.

Then, like a poor artist who never knows when the painting's done, he decides what a landscape needs is the scale provided by human figures.

Paints in Adam; as an afterthought, Eve.

What's wrong with this picture? he asks himself. Perhaps what is lacking is a proper perspective. And a little chiaroscuro wouldn't hurt.

He stands back from the easel, squints. Passes judgment. Throws down the brush.

Oh, hell, he sighs.

Mom and Dad

why is it, you must be dead
for us to want to know you?

you who walked with such a heavy tread
through our childhood?

pitting ourselves against you we became
champion arm-wrestlers, a bloodless

contest until the day we slammed your wrists
against the formica table and left home.

who were you, we wonder now.
when you were alive we never thought to ask.

we could pick you out in any line-up of moms and dads—
what else was there to know?

only now, staring at time-creased snapshots,
mementos of your holidays, do we wonder

who are those small figures almost lost
in a panoramic view of natural wonders?

who was that woman?
who was that man?

Lies

Beauty is truth,
truth beauty.

That's what you learn in school and then
          you graduate.

        Wonder why,
with beauty all around us for the taking,
this gross appetite for lies? Perhaps

        because
we drank them in with mother's milk
spiked with rosy futures, enriched
with happy endings. Perhaps

        because
we swallowed whole a father's
boastings–ignoring bitter

        off-stage laughter–

in which he cast himself
        as Gilgamesh,
        as Beowulf,
         as Roland at the pass,

then sent us off to
lovers who forswear their vows
every morning after.

(We might believe the children
had we not been children too
and remember our first mastery
was that of falsehood.)

Cat Woman

Living on an unpeopled planet
in the high altitude of old age
above the tree line of blood kin–
all dead, all dead, she says
when asked if she has family or friend–
she takes her station on the stoop
first day the super sends up steam.

Cats too, it would seem, clock summer's end
by that banging with a spoon against the tin
of tuna. From the wilderness of streets,
from under cars, from alleys slick
with garbage and empty lots composted
with dead leaves they come
from south, north, west, east,
padding to the feast.

Inside, through her open door, we can see
cans with openings as jagged as her pulse
like stepping stones on the crusty rug.
It is not so much the ammoniacal smell
lacquering the halls that offends us
as the orgies to be heard all winter long
through the thin walls.

Body Bag

I worked at Wal-Mart, in shipping,
flags everywhere in the parking lot.
Nine to five was the meat of my day
and I was fed up with being served
a thick slab of boredom, nothing
to do in this shitty town but get a crick
in the neck watching TV over the bar.

I wanted those special effects, the quick cuts,
the digitalized colors, life unreeling
with the rhythm of rap and something
happening every minute even it was
only a car crashing.

Don't blame them—I begged them to take me.
I wanted to be where the action was.
I was twenty-three.

Once a Woman

There was once a woman who called me daughter
but she is dead.

All my life
I have traveled
incognito
under
shifting aliases

matriculated,
attended no classes,
drifted
into jobs,
gave
false references,
quit
without notice–
all this
to confuse
the authorities.
No one found me out.

Fabricated
a husband,
posed
as the wife,
invented
two children
to call me
mother
yet

my door
stays closed
against
their pounding,
the husband
thumbs

through Dr. Spock,
croons:
honey! sweetheart!
are you there?
did you forget?

But his
are not
the love words
to turn this lock.

Even the landlord
I have outwitted.
An extra tenant
lives
under his roof
paying
no rent.
His spies are
everywhere:
checking
the radiators,
fixing
the plumbing.
He suspects
but
has no proof.
No one has found me out.

Then lo!
a masked man
starts probing
my teeth
and there
in the little
angled mirror
my mother's face.

I know it well—
that grimace
of disappointment,
her usual greeting.

He points
out decay
beneath
even rows
of porcelain caps.
I see her dentures.
There, he says,
is your pain.
I emerge
into the light
of day
numb
with novocaine
to flash
a smile
as sweet,
as fake
as hers
once looked to me.

I run I run I run
this marathon
of distancing.
Yet hard
on the staccato
beat
of my high heels
I hear
the slow
old-woman's shuffle
of slippered feet.

And I had thought
her dead.
She is marking
time
instead,
waiting
for the odds to even,
for me
to reach her age
as flesh-weary,
bone-tired
as she
so she can vent
her rage.

I only want you to be happy, she will say
and leave me bleeding.

Winter Solstice

Sad, this time of day,
the sky a crime scene,
a smear of red, bloody fingerprint
left behind, pale and smudged,
murderer's poor attempt
to wash it out. Darkness
comes, like the slow
leaching out of
consciousness,
the day done in.

Sad, this time of year,
winter seeping
down to bone, leaving
in frozen flesh the bruise
of former joy until
like those trees
barely remembering
the color green
you give up belief
in someone to
come home to.

Spring Cleaning

I am giving away
all these unfiled
photographs,
all these faces
once known,
never known
strangers all.

I am emptying
my closets
of clothes out-dated
out-grown.

I have scrubbed clean
the refrigerator
of moldy meals,
remnants of feasts
now poisonous.

Rugs taken up, walls bare,
how good
space unadorned
looks to me now.

Nothing is left
but to scour this writing.
No metaphors.

I search
for a simple line
of meaning limpid
as the eyes of that child
in the photograph
who once was me
which I just threw away . . .

About the Author

A Southerner by birth, Rebecca Kavaler has resided in New York City for longer than she admits. During that time, her short fiction has won various awards, including two National Endowment of the Arts fellowships and a New York State Council of the Arts grant. She has won the AWPA Award for Short Fiction and has appeared in *Best American Short Stories* and *Best of Nimrod.* Her stories are available in three collections, and her novel *Doubting Castle,* originally published by Schocken Books, was recently reprinted by Hamilton Stone Editions.

Her poetry has been published in *Atlanta Review, Fantasy & Science Fiction, Big Bridge, Hamilton Stone Review,* and *Prairie Schooner.*